The In-Between Places

Finding Peace in the Midst of Transition

DAVID L. MAHAN

ISBN 979-8-89243-228-3 (paperback)
ISBN 979-8-89243-229-0 (digital)

Christian Faith Publishing
832 Park Avenue
Meadville, PA 16335
www.christianfaithpublishing.com

Printed in the United States of America

Life is full of transition—predictable and capricious. It could be a salesperson waiting in that period of time between making their best pitch until the client makes the decision to buy or not to, or perhaps it's that time of rehab for an athlete who is recovering from a serious injury, all the while preparing for the hopeful return to the team next season. Sometimes it's more innocuous, as with a young child in "time-out" in their room, as a short-lived punishment, awaiting their chance to play outside again with their friends. Certainly, the growing-up years of any adolescent are significant periods of transition—in between the place of childhood and that of adulthood. Regardless of the reason for the transitional period, how we deal with it—responding with patience and a willingness to learn through it or fighting it every step of the way, resisting growth—will dictate how and when we come out on the other side of the "in-between place" of transition.

Section I

Chapter 1

Delayed Calling

One of life's greatest joys is discovering *what* we were created for, uniquely related to who we are, and the gifts and talents God has given us. It is that which gives purpose to our existence beyond the primary purpose of worshipping and knowing God. That "thing" that puts a bounce in our step, a song in our heart—a fulfillment of joy in our soul. Receiving a God-ordained calling in one's life is certainly a momentous occasion to be celebrated and cherished. But what happens when we receive that call or anointing by God to do something specific, and yet we discover the calling can't begin, let alone come to fruition, until much later? How does one cope with the much-avoided place called limbo?

Such was the case with King David in the Bible. We find in 1 Samuel that the prophet Samuel was told by God to anoint David as Israel's future king when he was only fifteen years old (most historians believe that was his age). Yet David did not step into that God-ordained role as king until he was thirty years old. For fifteen years, he had to wait, all the while knowing he was called by God to replace Saul as king. Although he ultimately reigned as king for forty years, those "in-between" years had to have been challenging, to say the least. How he responded to the time of waiting, without questioning or doubting, helped shape the type of king he would become.

In addition, what also defined King David was how he responded to Saul's quest to kill him prior to becoming king. In 1 Samuel 24:6–7, "David said to his men, 'The Lord forbid that I should do such a thing to my master, the Lord's anointed, or lift my hand against him; for he is the anointed of the Lord.' With these words, David rebuked his men and did not allow them to attack Saul. And Saul left the cave and went his way." By making that pivotal decision, despite whatever temptation he might have felt, David ultimately prevented what could have, in fact, expedited his claim to the throne.

Another staggering example is Abraham and the promised heir, Isaac. Between the time God gave Abraham (Abram) the promise that He would bless him (Abrahamic Covenant)—at the age of seventy-five, and make him into a great nation with infinitely numerous descendants—and when Isaac was born, twenty-five years had passed. During this extended period of time that elapsed, Abraham and his wife Sarah, motivated by impatience and doubt, made a terrible mistake that led to Ismael being born first. And consequently, a nation and religion was birthed, which is vehemently opposed to Israel to this day.

And let's not forget Moses, who had to wait forty years in the Midian desert before receiving the calling at the burning bush, thus fulfilling his God-given purpose of leading the Israelites out of slavery from Egypt. Like with Moses and David, there is an inner strength that comes from not only understanding but, more importantly, *remembering* the calling and trusting patiently in the Lord.

One must wonder if the cause for the delay, in some of the abovementioned instances, in seeing the calling come to fruition was, in fact, an intentional growing and testing season dictated by the Lord for a variety of reasons. Certainly, there is the benefit of strengthening as a result of waiting, "but they shall renew their strength who wait upon the Lord" (Isaiah 40:31). In the following, we will look at some of the more common reasons for the delay.

Discernment

Perhaps the smartest thing we can do, once we sense the Lord calling us to a specific task, is to engage a team of trusted friends and family to seek the Lord together for discernment and confirmation. All too often, we rush to the assumption we have heard the voice of God, only to discover what we heard was our own personal desires or goals. I realize that sometimes we get it right on our own, and we actually hear the Holy Spirit providing direction. The point being, there is nothing lost in asking those closest to us to come along and also pray for discernment and peace.

I believe the reason for reluctance here, certainly in my own life at times, is fear. What if they hear something different? This is where it is crucial to seek the right people to aid in the process—people who have demonstrated over time that they truly have a close and intimate relationship with the Lord and have proven that they hear from God clearly. We should never choose someone who will merely cater to our own predilections or selfish agendas. Also, it is crucial to remain open to possibly being wrong. In other words, don't let pride cloud your ability to receive what someone else is hearing from the Lord.

Patience is a critical necessity when going through the discernment stage. It is inherent for each of us to want to know the answer as fast as possible. Waiting can be an extremely challenging proposition. However, just as taking our time to do a job the right way the first time is prudent, thereby avoiding having to do it twice, so also taking the extra time at the beginning to ensure we are truly acting per the Lord's perfect will is well worth it in the end. The time we spend in the "in-between place" of consequence due to haste will always be a longer duration than simply waiting in advance for God-given discernment.

Character

Here we find what separates the sincerely earnest and devoted from the prideful and self-seeking. When trials and obstacles come our way, and they most certainly will, having genuine character and integrity will see us through those difficult and challenging times that can test our resolve and faith. Character, or wholeness, is an essential attribute that only God can provide. It is forged through the fire of adversity, honed through the sharpening that comes from a trusted friend (*see Proverbs 27:17*), and solidified over time and testing. Proverbs 11:3 says, "The integrity of the upright guides them, but the unfaithful are destroyed by their duplicity."

But how does character become developed? Obviously, it takes time and intentional effort to focus on areas in one's life that require growth, surrender, or correction. Humility is paramount to success in establishing character and integrity. If we truly desire growth, we must be open to instruction, advice, and discipline. Proverbs 15:22 tells us, "With many advisers, plans succeed." Therefore, we should always be open to counsel from a multitude of people that God has placed in our lives to provide adequate "sharpening." There is probably no other area where "living in the moment" is more crucial than during this time of refining fire.

Another key ingredient to developing character is learning. Learning from God's Word, learning from others whom God places in our path, and learning from our mistakes will all help mold our life into the "vessel of honor" that is sanctified and useful for the Master and prepared for every good work (*see 2 Timothy 2:15, 21*). True godly character will always stand out from the world's standards. We are called by God to be in the world, but *not of* the world. One litmus test that certainly proves our character has been refined by the Master's hand is when those whom we used to consider as friends now fall away from our life due to their own conscience and our convictions being incongruent.

Always remember, character, integrity, and honor are what we take with us from this life to our eternal life in heaven. If a relationship fails due to us growing closer to the Lord, then it's something we don't need to hang on to. God is to be our magnificent obsession and exceedingly great reward—nothing else!

Preparation

Oftentimes, the reason for the delay is God wanting to spend the appropriate time preparing the person for what lies ahead—the calling and purpose fulfilled. It is easy to imagine how costly and counterproductive it can be if the proper preparation is not embraced and achieved first. Imagine how terrible a pie would taste if the baker had not taken the necessary time kneading the dough and including the essential ingredients of sugar and spices. Or likewise, if the master carpenter didn't spend the required time in advance sharpening his tools and selecting the best pieces of wood to use to craft that fine piece of furniture.

God's timing and instructions are always perfect, and we must be mindful of that and do our part not to violate that by our own disobedience or resistance to the preparation needed. Be honest with yourself and with others regarding what still needs to be accomplished to be fully prepared. This is even more reason why ongoing prayer and intimate communication with the Lord is essential. That way, we can stay in step with the Holy Spirit's instruction, leading, and timing, ensuring that unnecessary detours and delays don't occur.

Surrender

Now the importance of surrendering to the Lord's will and timing is that we consciously acknowledge we don't have all the answers, and we don't know what's best—God alone does! Too often, we resist this stage in navigating the path through transition due to pride. We don't want to give up control or relinquish our right to make decisions. And all the while, we fail to remember only God is all-knowing and wiser than we could ever be. He is the master composer of our life's symphony.

One of my favorite stories is perhaps only a legend, but nonetheless, it is very provocative and inspiring.

The story states that a mother took her young son to a concert (most likely in the early 1900s) to hear the world-renowned Polish pianist Ignacy Jan Paderewski (1860–1941). During intermission, the mother was distracted, and the young boy slipped away and made his way up to the stage and sat down at the piano. Now the boy only knew how to play "Chopsticks," and so he started his own impromptu concert. Immediately, the crowd began to yell in disgust, outraged, and demanded the boy get off the stage. His mother, of course, was horrified, and she began to make her way up the steps of the stage to remove her disobedient son.

Before she could get that far, the master pianist, Paderewski, had heard the commotion, and he came up behind the young boy still playing the piano. Paderewski stretched his arms around the lad and began to compose a beautiful extemporaneous countermelody to "Chopsticks," all the while whispering in the boy's ear, "That's it. Keep playing. Don't stop. It's beautiful. You're doing great. I'm right here."

Now, after the surprise unsolicited encore ended, the crowd erupted in applause, and the boy left the stage beaming with joy and pride.

This story, whether fact or myth, is a beautiful picture of what God does for us during periods of transition in our life, if only we would listen to His whispering in our spirit, "Don't stop. Don't quit. Don't give up. Keep playing. Keep working. Keep remembering I'm right here by your side." And He is composing an amazing countermelody to our broken and imperfect attempt at the song called life!

While the period of transition was very brief for the young boy from when he found himself on the stage being scorned and chastised to when he exited the stage victorious and acclaimed, it is still the same as when we begin our period of transition to when it's over. The outcome will be determined by whether we exercise the courage to try and then listen to the Lord's encouragement and instruction with sweet surrender.

We find ourselves in great company when we consider the legends of the faith who have all experienced periods of transition—people such as Joseph, Daniel, David, Moses, Abraham, Samson, Jonah, and Mark, as well as Christ's disciples, especially Peter. Each of them had to wrestle with how they would endure and overcome, surrendering and trusting in God alone for strength and courage. Some certainly did better than others.

My favorite example (besides my namesake, David) is Joseph. Imagine being sold into slavery by your own siblings. Then, after having achieved a certain level of success in your new foreign home, you are falsely accused of wrongdoing and thrown in jail. Yet through it all, Joseph remained completely faithful to God, trusting in Him for protection, provision, favor, and vindication. One could clearly say all that Joseph endured was a test and none of his own doing. But despite Joseph having every right to complain and attempt to truncate his period of transition by whatever means possible, still, in the end, he didn't. He knew God had a plan and that he was in that uncomfortable place not without the Lord's knowledge and allowance. Joseph had learned early on the lesson we all need to embrace when we find ourselves stuck in the middle of transition. God is in control, and His timing is always perfect! The sooner we surrender and embrace what God wants us to learn, the sooner the perceived "curse" can become a rich blessing.

Sacrifice

What is the hardest thing in your life to sacrifice? I know, in my own life, it is time. Time is a very precious commodity, yet it is a gift from God. Just as with all the treasures God bestows upon us, we must be willing, without reluctance or complaining, to offer them back on the altar of sacrifice. It is as we make this outward demonstration that an inward reality of obedience is inculcated.

Abraham displayed arguably one of the best examples of sacrifice in the Bible next to our Lord and Savior Jesus Christ on the Cross. After waiting all those years for the promised heir, Isaac, to be born, God told Abraham to offer Isaac on the altar and sacrifice him. This was most certainly not a metaphoric sacrificing but, rather, a literal sacrifice—to the death!

Being a father and grandfather myself, I cannot even begin to imagine how Abraham managed to place his beloved son on that altar and begin to prepare him for death. However, praise God, another sacrifice was provided by the Lord, and the ram that was offered in Isaac's place was the reward for Abraham's willingness to obey God.

Sacrifice may not always be easy, but it leads to the life-giving presence and provision of God in our lives. It is as we pick our own "cross" daily and follow our Lord's example of sacrifice and surrender that we find the strength to endure and ultimately enjoy life victorious!

Chapter 2

Desert Detour

It was in the desert, the wilderness, that our Lord and Savior had to pass through a period of transition from the anointing, the baptism and blessing from the Father, to the fully activated and prophetic ministry leading to the culmination of the Cross. Here in the desert of transition, Jesus faced temptation. Although He came out on the other side victorious, of course, it was nonetheless a pivotal moment that prepared Him for what was to come next.

When we face temptation, what is our response? Is it one of utter dependence upon God for strength and resolve? Is it a time to quote Scripture for comfort and encouragement? Or is it a time we weaken and capitulate to the cravings of the flesh—that old sin nature? Perhaps crucifying the "flesh" daily, reminding oneself of the truth of Galatians 2:20 (NIV) would help: "For I have been crucified with Christ and I no longer live, but Christ lives in me.

The life I now live in the body, I live by faith in the Son of God, who loves me and gave Himself for me."

When a person knows where they're heading and eventually will be someday, and, more importantly, they know where they're going is, in fact, God's will, it makes waiting in the in-between place of transition more palatable and peaceful. However, the contrast being, when we initiate our own self-exiled elongated transition due to disobedience or haste, the process then is often full of bitterness and impatience and rife with discontent. In fact, I am writing this chapter from such a place of self-imposed exile and transition. In this place of waiting and wrestling with my own flesh, I am slowly learning the all-too-uncommon art of patience and contentment.

Acknowledging my own culpability for my current state of exile is the first step to learning that life-changing lesson. I accept the present circumstance for what it is—a consequence of my willful actions and disobedience. I am now learning from God what I need to embrace in order to grow through this temporal place of penance known as sustained solitude. Ironically, in my twenties and into my early thirties, I wanted (or at least thought I wanted) to permanently live in a cabin in the mountains, away from civilization—a recluse by choice. However, I was not entirely cognizant of what exactly I was asking for.

Since then, I have discovered that to be alone all the time is no better or healthier than to be surrounded by people 24/7. Just as God created us all with the inherent need for relationships, He also instilled in us, innately, the longing for times of quiet reflection, prayer, and worship that only solitude can provide. Balance is the key.

Now, some twenty-five years later, I have come to realize that life is a dance of balance executed upon the waters of change. The dance can be graceful, a thing of beauty for the onlooker to enjoy and glean from. Or the dance can be similar to a sophomoric attempt at coordination, all the while battling awkwardness, self-reliance, and disdain for the task at hand. If we take our "eyes of dependence" off Christ, the dance becomes similar to Peter's outcome. We sink fast.

The choice is really ours to make. How do we want to navigate the waters of change? In a manner worthy of admiration and praise or with regretful anguish? We must understand, the duration of transition is sometimes dependent upon that all-important decision. For if we choose the latter (regretful anguish), resisting the in-between place and refusing to grow and learn through it, then we may find ourselves with one "delayed departure" flight announcement after another. Rather, when we embrace where we are—not saying we have to love being there but still recognize we are there by God's sovereignty—and choose to learn and grow there, we often find the transition period is much shorter lived as well as beneficial.

White noise, such as self-serving distractions that keep us from hearing God's voice of direction and instruction, can be pernicious and certainly detrimental. Speaking of my own experience, when I was in my early forties, after finishing seminary, I sensed the Lord call me to Southern California for ministry. As I was still also working in construction, I had reason to periodically visit the Coachella Valley (Palm Springs area) for business. On one such occasion, shortly after I had decided to go back to Colorado to help a beloved family member during a rough period, I heard, in my spirit, the Lord tell me He would bring me back someday to that area in California. Not having lived there yet in the Palm Springs area, I thought it odd since the Los Angeles area was where I had been involved in ministry already. Nevertheless, I thanked the Lord for His faithful promise.

After only one year of being back in Colorado and helping my loved one deal with their situation successfully, I met my lovely wife. Having told her prior to matrimony about God's calling for me to go back to the Palm Springs area, and with her enthusiastic agreement and support, we were married. In a short time, God opened the door for us to move there to Palm Desert, California. We stayed there in the Coachella Valley for several years. However, as the enemy is so insidiously cunning, I found myself becoming more and more distracted by political life. And being very conservative myself, I soon found that I was having a hard time staying in a liberal state. Before even realizing what the ripple effect would be, I accepted a job offer, and we moved to Phoenix.

Long story short, I am now approaching the third year in Phoenix after having realized my act of disobedience and repented of my sin of arrogance and pride. The arrogance was thinking I knew what was best for me and my wife regarding where we should live. The pride was my rejecting my dear wife's respectful suggestion that we were to stay in the Palm Springs area.

I write this now humbled and, most of all, surrendered to the Lord's will. The house we bought in Phoenix is up for sale, and once it is sold, we will return to the place where God had called us initially. This time, I will be wiser and more focused on the calling for ministry and sedulously committed to avoiding those distractions and pitfalls, such as politics, that the enemy had previously used.

I am not suggesting that politics, in and of itself, is evil or wrong. Not at all. But for me, due to my own personality, it is a weakness that must be kept in check constantly. For some, the weakness may be alcohol or gambling, which the enemy also uses to keep a person off course and ineffective. The key is to discern what the weaknesses are and then to ask the Holy Spirit for wisdom to implement the proper measures to prevent them from detouring us into an unnecessary in-between place.

Life is too short and the future too uncertain and tenuous to waste precious time in a place of self-imposed exile. The children of Israel learned this lesson, albeit through multiple periods of exile. First were the forty years of wandering in the desert, awaiting entry into the promised land. Then exile and captivity under Assyrian rule, followed by exile under Babylonian captivity. Finally, after centuries of diaspora, the nation of Israel came into its own as the official State of Israel in 1948.

The important thing to remind ourselves continually while in a place of transition—whether ordained by God's will or due to our own free will—is that we are there because God, in His sovereignty, has allowed it, and He will, in turn, use it for His glory and our ultimate good. We should always find strength and comfort in Romans 8:28 (NIV), which states, "We know that in all things, God works for the good of those who love Him and have been called according to His purpose."

Doubt and confusion

It is astonishing how, when someone is stuck in the "desert place" of transition, perception can become a dangerous deception. An example from my own life is somewhat recent. I purchased land in Arizona a while back. The intent was to build a small second home there—a place specifically for prayer and writing. Having been in the construction industry myself for nearly forty years, I presumed being my own general contractor would be adequately realistic and easy. Unbeknownst to me at first, the ensuing delays in getting past certain milestone hurdles would result in a season of vacillating doubt, confusion, and uncertainty.

Being in a small town and given how busy the building industry is currently, finding subcontractor trade partners to bid, let alone perform the work, proved to be a much slower process than expected. Exacerbating the already frustrating situation was one simple fact. I am a person who is very fastidious, and I can be quite impatient at times. Insouciant I am not. Ironically, in my position as vice president of a construction company, I was personally involved in multiple projects that were more than ten million dollars in value each, whereas this personal second-home project had a mere one-hundred-thousand-dollar construction budget. An attitude adjustment and a resetting of my perspective could have saved me much stress and frustration.

A much older account of people allowing adversity to create room for dubious and confusing thoughts is the children of Israel and the exodus from Egypt led by Moses. In Exodus 16, we are told, "Then the whole community of Israelites began complaining again. They complained to Moses and Aaron in the desert. They said, 'It would have been better if the Lord had just killed us in the land of Egypt. At least there we had plenty to eat. We had all the food we needed. But now you have brought us out here into this desert to make us all die from hunger.'"

It is astonishing to think they would have missed out on the promised land and all the subsequent blessings from God if they had gotten what they asked for during that period of griping and giving up due to doubt and confusion.

Also, we find in the book of Joshua, chapter 7, because of one man's sin (Achan's), the people of

Israel faced humiliating defeat, and consequently, Joshua, their leader, faced confusion and doubt:

> But the Israelites were unfaithful in regard to the devoted things; Achan son of Karmi, the son of Zimri, the son of Zerah, of the tribe of Judah, took some of them. So the Lord's anger burned against Israel.
>
> Now Joshua sent men from Jericho to Ai, which is near Beth Aven to the east of Bethel, and told them, "Go up and spy out the region." So the men went up and spied out Ai.
>
> When they returned to Joshua, they said, "Not all the army will have to go up against Ai. Send two or three thousand men to take it and do not weary the whole army, for only a few people live there." So about three thousand went up; but they were routed by the men of Ai, who killed about thirty-six of them. They chased the Israelites from the city gate as far as the stone quarries and struck them down on the slopes. At this, the hearts

of the people melted in fear and became like water.

Then Joshua tore his clothes and fell facedown to the ground before the ark of the Lord, remaining there till evening. The elders of Israel did the same and sprinkled dust on their heads. And Joshua said, "Alas, Sovereign Lord, why did you ever bring this people across the Jordan to deliver us into the hands of the Amorites to destroy us? If only we had been content to stay on the other side of the Jordan! Pardon your servant, Lord. What can I say, now that Israel has been routed by its enemies? The Canaanites and the other people of the country will hear about this, and they will surround us and wipe out our name from the earth. What then will you do for your own great name?"

The Lord said to Joshua, "Stand up! What are you doing down on your face? Israel has sinned; they have violated my covenant, which I commanded them to keep. They have taken some of the devoted things; they have stolen, they have lied, they have put them with their own possessions. That is why the Israelites cannot stand against their enemies; they turn their backs and run because they have been made liable to destruction. I will not be with you anymore unless you destroy whatever among you is devoted to destruction.

"Go, consecrate the people. Tell them, 'Consecrate yourselves in preparation for tomorrow; for this is what the Lord, the God of Israel, says: There are devoted things among you, Israel. You cannot stand against your enemies until you remove them.'"

Our God is holy and righteous, and nothing that is unholy or defiled can stand in His presence. That is why the bloodstained Cross of Christ was, and is, of such profound importance. It alone makes us holy and acceptable in His sight. Also, an interesting aside, notice in the passage above how the Lord said, "*Israel* has sinned…*they* have violated my covenant. *They* have taken some of the devoted things; *they* have stolen." As is often the case, when we choose as an *individual* to disobey God, it can have a ripple effect impacting the lives of those around us also. As with Achan's rapacious act of disobedience, it certainly led to an ignominious outcome, which was visited on his family as well.

Disobedience

As in the case of the Israelites in the desert, the Bible tells us they were made to wander for forty years solely due to their disobedience. Now, before we get too "high on our horse" in critical judgment, we should take inventory of our own lives and examine the number of years we have felt were wasted because we couldn't simply obey what we knew God was telling us to do. The ending of the marriage we knew was a solemn covenant made, the failed ministry we were entrusted to shepherd, or perhaps it was the child we neglected to raise properly. I know, for myself, there have been unintended consequences because of my disobedience, which have led to years lost. I sincerely wish I could get them back still. Thank God for His promise in Joel 2:25 (NKJV), "I will restore to you the years that the swarming locust have eaten [*the years that were lost*]."

Now I am not suggesting we wallow in self-pity or self-condemnation. Living in the past never provides change. What does promote change is *learning* from the past and being resolved in our heart and mind never to repeat those same mistakes again. We should remember, eventually, the children of Israel did enter the promised land. They did see victory and, centuries later, realized the fulfillment of their nation.

What is it that makes one prone to disobey? Certainly, it could be multiple reasons. However, I believe the core precipitating cause is arrogance and pride. It's when we believe (or, rather, deceive ourselves) that we know best—that God must be wrong. That's when disobedience is born. The very first example of this was in the garden of Eden when Adam and Eve listened to the wrong voice (the deceiver).

One of the most assured ways we can prevent disobedience is by humbling ourselves daily, reminding that "inner man" that we are broken and imperfect. That we are in desperate need of a Savior. It is stating the obvious: that only God alone is perfect and omniscient. His ways are always best and lead to life! That is what keeps our "old sin nature" in check and submitted to His Lordship in our lives. God alone has the words of life. Where else could we go?

Duplicity

The true definition of *duplicity* is "deception, double-dealing, dishonesty, and double-mindedness." Here, the guilty party for any deception is twofold. First, and most obvious, it is the enemy of people's souls: Satan, the "father of lies." However, the person is equally to blame sometimes. Given the power of the human mind, we are more than capable of making ourselves believe any lie or falsehood. It is quite sobering to think how many times we might be missing out on God's very best plan for our lives simply because we chose not to exercise faith; instead, we sold ourselves a lie that came straight from the pit of hell.

There is also the aspect of duplicity that is a direct result of not being able to make up one's own mind and stick to something. Here, the person with wanderlust is most prone to duplicity. Perhaps it can be appropriate in certain seasons of life to be laid-back and not have any real concrete plans and just go with the flow. However, in relation to realizing that specific purpose for which you were created and working sedulously toward seeing it come to fruition, there is no room for being lackadaisical or indifferent.

Whether it's an effect of dishonesty or double-mindedness, the result is the same. We miss out on the life we were intended to live. Therefore, if one wishes to step into that calling or anointing from the Lord, then one must remain steadfast with a single-minded laser focus and stay the course! Speaking of this truth, "then we will no longer be like infants, tossed back and forth by the waves, and blown here and there by every wind of teaching and by the cunning and craftiness of people in their deceitful scheming" (Ephesians 4:14 NIV).

Here again, we find great reason for having trusted confidants in our life who can watch us and, if needed, call us out on any double-mindedness they see. It is an extremely insidious strategy of the enemy to trick us into thinking all we're doing is looking at various options or simply being open-minded when, in fact, sometimes, what we're doing is trying to renegotiate the deal. In other words, our CEO,

God Almighty, Creator of the universe, has given us our marching orders. He has instructed us, perspicuously, on where we are to go and how we are to get there. Yet, in our presumptuous arrogance, we think we know what's best. We couldn't be more wrong!

Death of the vision

Proverbs 29:18 says, "Where there is no vision, the people perish." But what leads to the vision's death in the first place? Perhaps it is a lack of concentration and focus or maybe a lack of resolve. It could also be as simple as a failure to remember. This is one area where Orthodox Judaism and Orthodox Christianity excel—the faithfulness to remind each person and their descendants of the promises and faithfulness of God. To remain unwavering in the recollection of centuries of God's covenant with His people. This is certainly the stalwart anchor of their faith and, quite frankly, should be of the Evangelical Christian faith as well.

In Psalm 103, David reminds us to "praise the Lord, my soul, and *forget not* all His benefits." Also, it was David who wrote, "I will tell of *all* Your wonderful deeds, oh Lord" (Psalm 9:1). We should always take the time to recount all the many blessings God has entrusted us with. There is great power and release in declaring the Lord's sovereignty, generosity, and faithfulness! This is our greatest weapon in keeping the vision alive.

One of the most pernicious dangers we find in the in-between place of transition, or even simply restoration, is becoming content to stay there. The trappings of what's familiar, comfortable, and easy can swiftly and subtly motivate us to trade the promised land of vision for the desert of complacency. Even wanting to stay longer than we should in that mountaintop retreat and, consequently, resisting the obedient act of returning to the valley below, where God wants to use us (the vision), is an all-too-common phenomenon.

I suppose this is relatively similar to what has happened to some kidnapping victims, known as Stockholm syndrome. The precipitating event might be very different; however, the end result is noticeably the same. It is the desire to remain in a place of captivity, exile, or retreat even though a person has gained their freedom and marching orders to advance. Undoubtedly, the emotional ties to what has become so familiar and even secure can become the very chains that preclude someone from living the life they were meant to live.

On a much larger scale is the analogous example of a Christian's view on life in this world versus eternal life in heaven. What is meant to only be seen as temporal, merely leading up to our final and eternal destination, oddly transforms into the central theme of focus. Heaven—with all its glory, perfection, and peace—takes a back seat to what some inevitably pursue with all their energy and attention, life here and now, simply because it's what they know and can see.

Not to be overly critical, but this is what I believe happened during the forty years of wandering in the desert for the children of Israel following their freedom from four hundred years of captivity. While I certainly am convinced they wanted their freedom and subsequent inheritance in the promised land, the desert became, for them, what was familiar and, in turn, safer to remain in than entering the new and unknown promised land of Canaan. After scouting out what was across the Jordan River, only two of the twelve men were confident in advancing. The remainder saw only giants in their way as obstacles. Tragically, in the end, what is safe and familiar can never yield as much joy and peace as what God has promised in the unchartered and wild frontier of His divinely ordained vision.

We must press into the secret place of intimacy with God, especially when in the place of transition. It is imperative to seek His face continually with all our heart, soul, and strength. God promises us in Jeremiah 33:3 (ESV), "Call to me and I will answer you, and will tell you great and hidden things that you have not known."

Prayer is the key to understanding why we are in a place of transition and what we need to learn to grow through it. God has all the answers. He alone is all-knowing. It is His heart's desire to teach us and reveal His plan and purpose for us. Remember, prayer is the vessel that carries us to the other shore across the waters of transition and trial.

Section II

Chapter 3

Mistaken Identity

There are many reasons people can "lose themselves" in life, whether through divorce, an abusive or codependent relationship, an unholy obsession, or due to an addiction. While the precipitating event is widespread, the steps to "finding oneself" can be somewhat comparable. The first step is to recognize the need for assistance and recruit help from the appropriate person or persons. Let's start with recovery and restoration from an addiction.

Never having suffered from an addiction such as gambling or alcohol or drugs, I have to share the following solely from what I have learned talking with others about their journey and, of course, from what I believe the Lord wants me to say. First, I must start by saying that this portion was written with the utmost compassion. I believe the greatest tactic the enemy uses to ensnare a person into an addiction is a lie crafted in the pit of hell. Undoubtedly, there is often a precipitating event that becomes the impetus to make a person want to escape reality. Certainly, drugs, alcohol, and pornography are examples of such addictions that serve as an escape mechanism.

Speaking of the lie from hell, perhaps it's a belief that one can never achieve a truly fulfilled sex life within the sanctity of marriage (hence, the addiction to pornography) or perhaps the feeling of peace and euphoria could never come from something as simple as prayer and worship (hence, the abuse of drugs or alcohol). The lie could also be that we will never get ahead and be successful enough merely from hard work and determination. Therefore, what is, for some, simply a form of innocent entertainment, such as gambling, becomes, for others, an addictive behavior that can lead to financial ruin.

Whatever the deception, the big illusion is that we must somehow take control of the situation ourselves to achieve the desired end result because we cannot trust anyone else—not even God. This was the ultimate lie that Satan fed Adam and Eve in the garden: "Did God really say that…and you will not certainly die" (Genesis 3).

The implied deceitful message here is that the first residents of earth should not trust their Creator. The painfully perpetual result was mankind being evicted from paradise and sentenced to the longest in-between place of transition ever!

This is why John 8:32 is of such paramount importance for us to remember each and every day: "You shall know the truth, and the truth shall set you free." It is in that place of revelation from God, through His Spirit, that we learn who we really are and what we were created to accomplish. However, sadly, addictions always rob us of that realization—if we allow them to. I believe it all starts with our thoughts. The battlefield is in our mind, as the Bible tells us in 2 Corinthians 10:3–6, "Take every thought captive and make it obedient unto Christ."

As my dad used to say, "We can't keep the birds from flying over our heads, but we can sure keep them from building nests in our hair." Negative and destructive thoughts and lies from the enemy will come our way, but we have the life-changing power in the Risen Christ to ignore and repudiate those insidious tactics.

Of course, addictions are not the only thing the enemy uses to cause us to lose ourselves. Quite often, it can be accomplished through a dysfunctional and codependent relationship. We take on a role we were never created to play, just like an actor pretending to be someone they are not. Although the motivation for this disguise is noble and perhaps even selfless, in the end, we are not only depriving ourselves of living life on honest terms, but we are also doing the other codependent recipient a grave disservice. Instead of recognizing the warning signs early on and avoiding those unhealthy, unspoken agreements made because of a desperate need for love, affection, or security, we capitulate our freedom to be who God created us to be in order to placate or appease a spouse, a boss, or perhaps even a parent.

Again, let me reiterate. This is not meant as a critical or captious form of judgment. But rather, I am speaking to myself as well in a sincere hope to affect healing, recovery, and freedom.

As I was growing up, my father (whom I loved very much and was extremely close to) had a debilitating chronic illness, which lasted for most of my childhood. It wasn't until a year before my parents' death, when I was already grown, that my dad was healed physically from his ailment. During those years of my youth though, my sisters and I took on, in various ways, a certain codependency to deal with the fear and uncertainty of our father's plight. For me, it meant becoming a perfectionist in every sense so as not to burden my mother, or father, with any unnecessary added stress. This perfectionist mindset, coupled with the unbridled fear that my dad could die at any time, led to an unmitigated desire for everything to be predictable and within my control. Hence, rigid expectations were born.

Or maybe it's through an obsession we can't seem to master and bring under control that we discover we are operating under a mistaken identity. For example, those of us who have struggled with OCD for any length of time will tell you reality becomes distorted and trusting becomes a very scary proposition. There, in that place of fear, we lose sight of our true God-given identity of being strong in the Lord and in the power of His might. We fail to remember, all too often, "that God did not give us a spirit of fear—but of power, love, and a *sound mind*" (2

Timothy 1:7). His perfect love casts out all fear (1 John 4:18)!

Triage

Just like in a hospital's emergency room, where there are highly trained professionals who can immediately ascertain what the patient's medical situation is and the required appropriate treatment, so also, when we humbly ask for help from a professional counselor or minister, we are stating we don't know what's best but are willing to trust that God will, through that person, provide the much needed triage for our soul.

Remember, one of the Lord's names is Wonderful Counselor. Who better to seek help from?

No person in their right mind would refuse to go to the emergency room at a hospital if they had a severed finger or perhaps had been accidentally shot while on a hunting excursion. That person would know immediately that the best course of action is to seek professional help from trained medical experts. Likewise, if someone knows they are sinking fast in the quicksand of addictive and destructive behavior, they should recognize their only true hope is to seek God's divine help and supernatural healing—often through the assistance of a person trained and educated in providing mental and emotional healing.

It is only in that setting that wisdom and discernment can be applied to ascertain what the root cause is for the affliction of the soul. Self-medicating for such a dilemma is extremely dangerous—nugatory, to say the least. Time is of the essence when it comes to evaluation of the crisis and the subsequent treatment needed.

Rehab

Rehabilitation can be a very long and tedious journey. Often, it is nonlinear; that is to say, there are ups and downs throughout the process. While a person may take two steps forward, they may also take one step back. What I believe is the most valuable ingredient to successful recovery is consistency and transparency. Allowing oneself to become accountable to others, being worthy of that trust, and committing to a clearly established plan of consistent therapy will yield the very best results possible. This part of the journey can take longer than desired and will, in turn, precipitate numerous times of temptation to give up. We mustn't allow that to happen. Again, here's a great opportunity for the loved ones to surround us with encouragement and love and to cheer us on to completion. Just as Cortez told his men in 1519 to burn the ships when they began to grumble and complain about the New World, so also must we "burn the ships" of our past destructive habits and addictions and resolve never to go back to that old life again!

Discovery

As I mentioned earlier, I was very close to my dad. As I grew to be a man, we came to enjoy a relationship as best friends, as well as father and son. Our common interests and hobbies, like-minded perspective on life, and same faith and deeply held beliefs were even more consistent with what one might expect to find with two brothers. It was truly a beautiful life-giving relationship.

Years after my parents' untimely death in a car accident, I began to notice I had been dealing with an ongoing and increasingly frequent symptom of anger brought on by criticism, mostly of myself but certainly directed at others also. Expectations, in turn, plagued my life that neither I nor anyone else could ever live up to—let alone life, in its capricious nature, ever satisfy. So I decided to see a Christian counselor. This counselor was quite proficient in knowing exactly what questions to ask to prompt my own self-examination and introspective analysis.

It was after one of those sessions, when I had stopped at a restaurant on my way home for dinner, that a life-changing experience took place. As I sat at the table by myself, looking out the window at the beautiful rugged mountain peaks in the Phoenix area, I sensed I was suddenly not alone.

I realize this may sound strange, but it was as if Jesus sat down next to me at the table. And with the Holy Spirit dwelling inside me already, I heard the Lord ask a surprisingly poignant question. He said, "What if your dad made a mistake? What if he didn't establish the best of boundaries, although he had the best of intentions? What if his intensely fervent zeal to be a pastor fulltime, as well as working at GM for twenty-five years, albeit very honorable, took its toll on his health, which contributed to his debilitating illness?"

At that moment, as I allowed myself to entertain those thoughts as reality for the first time, through the lens of constructive criticism, and let them marinate in my soul, it was as if my dad was sitting there at the table as well, telling me it was okay to think that way of him. That the God-given postulation, which I would never have even dared think before over the past forty-five years, was the truth. And the truth was setting me free!

Suddenly, I felt a tidal wave of freeing emotion filled with peace and surrender come washing over me to the point I couldn't contain it any longer. After I got up and went to the men's room, where I had a time of emotional release, I came back to the table a new man, transformed by God's grace and revelation. All the while, I still loved my dad just as much and honored his memory and legacy the same as before.

Since that epiphany experience occurred, inspired by simply being open to asking some tough questions, I have experienced liberating freedom from overly critical and captious thoughts and attitudes. It was as if the minor criticism I had suppressed for over forty years, refusing to see my dad as anything less than almost perfect, had finally been directed to the appropriate place. And now I no longer needed to redirect those suppressed attitudes elsewhere, as in some sort of misguided transference.

I share all that to say, perhaps our perception of the past is what's keeping us from experiencing breakthroughs in the present and, in turn, freedom to move forward and live a life full of peace and joy, no longer stranded in the in-between place. This is an instance where recruiting others around oneself to seek the Holy Spirit's wisdom and discernment is crucial. The imperative need for the "counsel of community" is intensified by the likelihood that the person who is navigating the waters of transition may not be able to see the horizon ahead of or behind them clearly.

Restitution

Now this part may hurt a little. When we have lived any length of time in destructive addictions or dysfunctional relationships, there can certainly be collateral damage inflicted on those around us. One example is a drug addict who has stolen from a family member to support their habit. Upon being delivered from that addiction and restored by God's grace to a life free and whole, he/she may need to at least try to repay the family member for the offense and rebuild the trust violated. Certainly, there could be those who will not be receptive to that effort. And in those cases, it is best to at least communicate remorse and ask for forgiveness.

If nothing else, this important stage of recovery will serve to destroy the proclivity for shame to become a stronghold. In this author's opinion, the cure for shame is honesty. Secrets are the breeding ground for shame. Therefore, when we openly admit our failures and the pain we have caused someone else and seek to make amends, we can experience freedom from the chains of disgrace and shame.

The Bible tells us in John 8:12 (NIV), "When Jesus spoke again to the people, He said, 'I am the light of the world. Whoever follows me will never walk in darkness but will have the light of life.'" And 1 John 1:7 (NIV) states, "And if we walk in the light, as He is in the light, we have fellowship with one another, and the blood of Jesus, His Son, purifies us from all sin." The light of Christ in our lives will dispel all the darkness of shame. And then the truth of who we were yet no longer are (since we are new creations in Christ)—that is what sets us free indeed!

Now walk forward in that light and truth, confident that Christ will walk with you, empowering you to do the work of restitution. Don't be afraid to ask the offended or betrayed party what their experience was like and what their current feelings are toward you. Then be willing and open to truly hear the sometimes-brutal truth. Whatever you do, don't make excuses. Don't argue with them about their experience or recollection. Just listen. Then, when it's appropriate, say you're sorry and truly mean it. Tell them, while you don't expect their forgiveness, you certainly hope they can forgive you someday. It is only in that place of sharpening that honest feedback, as much as it may hurt and be uncomfortable, will provide the stepping stones to restitution and lasting recovery.

God's waiting room

The reason for this portion's name is because it is more directed toward the family members and friends of the person dealing with the transition. All too often, when a person is suffering from an addiction or abusive relationship, they tend to bifurcate their life into separate areas—the motivating purpose to keep others shielded from the truth. Their intent may or may not be noble and selfless; however, regardless of their reasons, the people closest to them, who love and care for them the most, end up being hurt and alienated.

On the contrary, when we let those people in and share the struggle with them, they can, in turn, become privy to updates of progress and recovery while remaining in "God's waiting room." Just as in a hospital's waiting room, where loved ones are readily available for the doctor's periodic status updates, when a loved one knows the circumstances and situation, they can pray strategically and receive instruction and encouragement from the Lord. Unfortunately, when we have cultivated an environment of reticent behavior and poor communication with our loved ones and God, it can become a significant hindrance to healing and restoration.

Regarding another reason, we so often want to avoid "worlds colliding," so we keep our loved ones at arm's length when what we desperately need is their support. Perhaps the following is the culprit. We could be afraid of rejection, judgment, or condemnation. The shame and guilt one already feels due to the chronic addiction and the inability to sever those chains of bondage has become the compelling force that rejects, as a sort of pre-emptive strike, the very community where healing and deliverance could be waiting. But what if we're wrong? What if the very people out in the waiting room are, in fact, the very agents of God's healing, compassion, and supportive encouragement who, if allowed in, could help facilitate an accelerated transition? Remember, it is in God's presence where we discover our true identity.

The following suggestion is directed at both the person experiencing the transition and the loved one waiting on the sidelines. Ask yourself this question. What if the world, or at least your sliver of it, were coming to an end in one hour, and you knew you were going to die and couldn't stop it? What would you do in that one last hour? Who would you call or go see? What would you say? Now go and do it. Those actions, good deeds, or words spoken might not necessarily end your present stay in the in-between place of transition. But then again, it might. Either way, what you just did or said was probably of significant eternal value and importance.

Agitating Aging

Ever hear someone say "growing old sure is hard," only to hear the response, "it sure beats the alternative." Certainly, the latter part of that adage is the one to embrace as reality. I am not saying growing old isn't difficult at times; anyone who has passed that mid-century benchmark understands that to be true. What I am inferring is that we need to thank God for every day we get to live with those we love and to do that which we love doing. But what is that which we love doing? That is an imperative question I had to ask myself about a year ago.

After nearly forty years in construction and having never felt passionate about it, I was faced with a vexing conundrum. Do I keep working in a field I have never enjoyed for the next ten years, or do I find my true calling? Oddly enough, in January of 2023, I sensed the Lord was telling me to write a book called *Covenant with God.*

It was truly a labor of love, focused on our nation returning to the covenant our Founding Fathers made with the Almighty when this nation was born. I loved every minute of the writing process, as well as the editing process with my publisher.

As a result of my obeying God, I realized my true calling. Apart from being a worshipper of God, it was to be a writer. It was a gift I had sensed even as an adolescent, when I won first place in a one-act playwriting contest in school. Then, after my parents' death, I wrote numerous poems, which was very therapeutic. However, the many ensuing years of living life, working hard, paying the bills, raising my son, and going to seminary—it all seemed to precipitate my unconscious suppression of that gift and passion.

After completing the first book, I have written a few others. And I have proven what my father always told me to be true: "Do what you truly love doing for a living, and you'll never work a day in your life!" I have literally redefined myself and am looking forward to the "golden years" with great anticipation.

I share all that to say, it's never too late to reinvent yourself and make a positive change that will make you feel young again. Age really is relative (as my wife keeps telling me), and I have come to believe that. Therefore, search your heart, pray, and ask those closest to you for insight and revelation as to what that passion might be that gives you ebullience and hope for the years to come. After all, the old saying "the future is not certain" goes both ways. In other words, while we don't know if we'll be here on earth tomorrow, we also don't know if we'll be around for perhaps twenty or thirty or forty more years to come. All the more reason to not delay or compromise. Life is too precious and capricious not to spend every day honoring those God has placed in your journey and honoring God, most of all, by doing that which you were created to do.

Trust me. Once you discover that passion and calling and step into it fully, you will find the agitation of aging start to vanish and the misconception you must accept the status quo dispelled. This will, in turn, facilitate the transition period of aging to be filled with peace, joy, and contentment.

Chapter 4

Frustrating Failures

Everyone throughout the course of living will experience failure. After all, to err is human. And while failure is to be expected, most people desire and strive to mitigate failure as much as possible. But what happens when a person has a reoccurring theme of failure, especially in a specific area of their life? This unwanted place of perpetual transition between trial and success can leave a soul discouraged and dubious about the future.

Having said that, I want to stress that a person should never avoid taking chances and moving forward toward an earnest goal for fear of failure. Theodore Roosevelt, one of our nation's greatest presidents, said it best:

> It is not the critic who counts; not the man who points out how the strong man stumbles, or where the doer of deeds

48

could have done them better. The credit belongs to the man who is actually in the arena, whose face is marred by dust and sweat and blood; who strives valiantly; who errs, who comes short again and again, because there is no effort without error and shortcoming; but who does actually strive to do the deeds; who knows great enthusiasms, the great devotions; who spends himself in a worthy cause; who at the best knows in the end the triumph of high achievement, and who at the worst, if he fails, at least fails while daring greatly, so that his place shall never be with those cold and timid souls who neither know victory nor defeat.

Certainly, the case of persistent or reoccurring failure in a particular "arena" can be vexing as to the reason why success is so elusive. However, as the Rough Rider stated so aptly, failure while "daring greatly" always separates oneself from the company of "timid souls." Better to have tried and failed than never to have tried at all.

And while there may be great comfort in the abovementioned exhortation from the former president, still, anyone who has experienced this relentless attempt to succeed, only to face failure again and again, knows all too well the anguish of unrest. The unyielding quest to understand what one is doing wrong can sometimes only be answered in the familiar setting of community. Here again, we find the absolute necessity for inviting those closest, who know us best, into a loving circle of confidence and trust.

All too often, the one who is failing repeatedly becomes callous and unable to discern the reason why—mostly due to the cloud of frustration obscuring any revelation. Although, when family and friends who care for and understand us best are brought into the equation, illumination often becomes accessible. The key is to remain open to receiving their insight and counsel. If one truly desires to be liberated from the holding cell of elongated transition, then they must be willing to recruit and accept wise counsel from objective vantage points. As mentioned earlier in this book, Proverbs 15:22 tells us, "With many advisers, plans succeed."

Fortuitous for the sojourner through transition is the companion who has already experienced a similar struggle and has emerged victorious. Here, a shared lesson learned can make all the difference between giving up and pressing on. We must always be mindful of what present challenges we are facing can be used later in God's perfect timing to encourage and bolster someone else. The key is to see life, in general, as a shared journey with multiple entrance and exit points where others will walk alongside us, giving and receiving assistance. This perspective is how we begin to experience serendipity at its best.

It is quite ostentatious when a person who hardly ever experiences failure flaunts their success. That is certainly not the type of companionship we need when making the trek along the rugged peaks and valleys of repeated failure. Rather, what we need is a humble servant who has compassion yet understands and wields efficacious encouragement and motivation. Tough love in the appropriate setting is sometimes required.

I had a dear friend, many years ago in Colorado, who was middle-aged and had a propensity to failure in predominantly one area: self-confidence. He would repeatedly put himself down due to all the times he had tried to succeed in his life but could never seem to get ahead. By the time I met him, he was already haunted by past mistakes and was completely fear-ridden. Shame had taken hold and created a self-fulfilling prophecy in his mind that kept him from taking any more chances. He had resigned himself to accept his plight as some type of self-deprecating penance for the sins of his youth. I tried repeatedly to convince him that was a lie coming straight from the pit of hell, but still, he insisted a victorious life's testimony would never be his to enjoy.

Finally, I realized that although my intentions were admirable, the outcome was ineffective. The reason, I ascertained, was due to my belief that he needed to be treated gingerly and with the utmost compassion. And while compassion was appropriate, as is usually the case, sometimes it needs to be blended with tough love. Once I realized this and implemented a different approach, encouraging him but also providing admonishment and stern rebuke for his defeatist attitude, I began to see a new man emerge. It seemed that all his life, he had been coddled by his parents when what he desperately needed was someone he trusted and admired to take a firm stance and insist he change his mindset.

Soon I had the distinct pleasure of witnessing his success in various areas of his life—relationally and financially. His story is more ubiquitous than we want to realize or admit. There are hosts of people who simply need a friend or loved one to come alongside and, instead of holding their hand, place their hand on the plow and help them push.

The longer I live, the more I am convinced that our failures need not define us or direct us. Instead, we should always allow the One who created us and knows us best to define who we are and who we were created to be. And then we should embrace the Christlike counsel from those He places in our path, and we should stop keeping score of past failures. Instead, take a hard realistic look at what is truly worth the effort and within the realm of our God-ordained calling. This is one way we will see the transition period of failure truncated. And, in turn, we learn to grow through the painstaking process of defeat into victory.

Section III

Chapter 5

Ghostly Grief

Complicated loss

Loss is never easy to endure or welcomed. However, there certainly are times when loss occurs, and with it comes an immediate sense of understanding and even acceptance. An example would be an elderly member of the family passing away in their sleep, who has lived perhaps ninety years or more and had a wonderfully loving and fruitful life. In such an instance, while there is still sadness and grief experienced, the loss can be accepted relatively soon and the life of the loved one celebrated with joy.

Sadly, that is not the case when a child dies, whether due to an accident or disease or for any reason. And certainly, this same type of complicated loss is precipitated by a messy divorce or perhaps being unexpectedly let go from a long career. At times like these, it takes much longer to understand the reasons (if at all), and acceptance can be a long and drawn-out process as well (if even possible). How one deals with this kind of painfully protracted and confusing grief is predicated upon various factors.

The reason for the seemingly strange name of this chapter is due to how ghosts (if one believes they exist) tend to linger as a result of "unfinished business." I am certainly not advocating for the existence of such spectral beings. However, I am implying that grief oftentimes can linger beyond what is commonly expected. Albeit different for each person, the duration of the grieving process can be extended if there is an unresolved issue or business that was not attended to prior to death.

One of those factors might be the status of the relationship one had with the deceased prior to the loss. Another extenuating circumstance could be how much time there was, if any, to prepare and say good-bye. Regardless of any amount of time allowed for preparation or farewells, complicated loss will usually be accompanied with regret and what-ifs. Regret is certainly a ghost that haunts from within and is quite often difficult to evict. The "exorcism" process can entail several various courses of action.

One such step might involve writing a letter to the deceased. I realize that sounds strange, but it sometimes helps to articulate what you should have said or meant to say when the loved one was still alive. Another course of action that I personally found to be helpful when my parents died was to write poems that described my feelings toward them that I never got around to communicating and issues in our relationship that were unresolved. Writing such sentiments down on paper (or in your computer) is a wonderful way to reflect later on the growth and resolution that has transpired over time. Be honest with how you truly feel. Write what you would say if they were sitting in the room with you. Don't be concerned with syntax or structure; just express your heart toward them. Do it with the confidence that the words have the power to affect change—which they do. Remember, words have the power of life and death (*see Proverbs 18:21*).

Now, as we pass through the various stages of grief, the important thing to remember is that everyone processes and experiences grief uniquely. Therefore, one may linger in the denial stage for an extended period of time yet hardly even realize there is a stage called bargaining. Another may accept the loss immediately, bypassing denial altogether, yet spend what seems like an eternity dealing with the desolate fog of depression.

Grief is an impetus in and of itself. It cannot be reasoned or negotiated with. We stand no chance of placating its symptoms or appeasing its origin. Whatever control we may perceive we have, in the end, our capitulation to the journey is all that is within our power.

As with all manifestations of transition one can experience in life, the crucial truth to understand is while regret is very real sometimes, it can usurp one's energy and strength with very little (if any) return on the time wasted. I do not mean to sound insensitive. My own life has been rife with regret at times, but I have learned the hard way, it is a ghost that haunts from within and offers no constructive counsel. Instead, we should learn from our past mistakes and failures and then leave those mistakes and failures where they belong: in the past. Carrying them around with us, like a prisoner's ball and chain, in the present only serves to take up valuable space in our soul where joy, peace, and contentment are waiting to abide.

Grief is certainly neither linear nor perspicuous. It is messy, erratic, and confusing at times. Its capricious nature is a taskmaster that can leave one emotionally drained and discouraged. However, it is to our advantage, as the sojourner through the valley of grief, not to try and change our own experience of the journey or have expectations of how it should look and feel. But rather, embrace it and lean into the process, understanding, as we do, the duration of the journey will most likely be shorter lived and perhaps even more meaningful in the end. As the old saying goes, "resistance is futile."

Instead of presuming to convey any form of description of the various stages of grief (denial, anger, bargaining, depression, and acceptance), allow me to simply offer one additional piece of advice. Loss, and its ensuing by-product of grief, is a part of life. And while our Lord promised us there will be pain along life's journey, He also promised to never leave or forsake us. If we will only receive His comfort and peace in the midst of life's darkest times, we can and will come through the other side stronger, wiser, and closer to God.

Darkness pending

The impending death of either a loved one or oneself is an extremely arduous and painful experience to process and navigate through. Certainly, it is deserving of the utmost compassion. Uniquely different from the death of a loved one who has already passed, anticipated death is rife with mixed emotions and ambivalent feelings. Watching someone we deeply care for, and love, suffer through the agonizing trauma and anguish of a fatal illness is an experience never to be forgotten.

I believe the key here is to try to focus on the opportunity to communicate and express feelings of love, appreciation, and affirmation to the appropriate person or persons rather than focusing on the impending loss. I realize this is much easier said than done, and due to my parents' type of passing, I was spared this turbulent experience. However, expressing these feelings while still possible is an opportunity that, if missed, could lead to regret for many years to come. Obviously, this is the most important question to be asked: Is one confident of where they will spend eternity? The famous cliché "seize the day" could never be more relevant than here or more urgent than now.

Here, I believe, the ministry of presence is of the utmost value. Too often, we feel uncomfortable, not knowing what is best to say, so we end up avoiding the person who desperately wants and needs our comforting presence. I learned early on when my parents died that after the funeral and burial was over and all the subsequent business affairs were resolved, the family and friends who lingered still and were simply present just to sit with me were what helped me navigate my grief more than anything else.

Therefore, if the grief is impending yet not fully imposed, the willingness to devote your time and your presence could be the very tonic of peace and comfort they desperately need.

Wounded grief

The grief process can become thwarted and, in turn, slow down the transition period, resulting in delayed healing and acceptance. Certainly, if there were unresolved issues with the departed such as unforgiveness, harsh words spoken, betrayal, or abandonment, then unless those things are rectified and resolved somehow, the wound of grief will never fully heal.

I am not speaking of a healing that involves forgetfulness—neither of the offense nor the loss. Only God has the ability to throw our transgressions in the "sea of forgetfulness—as far as the east is from the west." What I am referring to is a healing of acceptance: of wholeness. It is a healing that results in a true inner peace that passes all understanding. Again, as mentioned in earlier chapters, communication is key. Although the person may be gone from this world, you are still here. And you must find a way to reach closure, accept the loss, and attain lasting peace. Otherwise, the unfinished business could be a ghost that haunts from within your soul.

When I was only nine years old, I took a dare from a neighborhood kid at our local playground and slid down a giant steel "spider" with a two-foot-long section missing in one of the spider's legs. The resulting injury of me falling through that missing section of steel was my chin ripped wide open and, consequently, almost twenty stitches. Upon reaching my home, with the bottom of my face gushing blood profusely, my mother proceeded to force my head under the kitchen sink and began scrubbing the wound to clean it. Let me assure you, the pain was excruciating, and it was a good thing I hadn't learned yet all the swear words I know today as an adult.

Yet as painful as that process was, the doctor informed my mom at the hospital that the healing process of my soon-to-be-scarred chin would be accelerated due to her meticulous efforts. Cleaning a wound is hardly ever pain-free. However, the end result is well worth the momentary trauma.

I believe grief is probably the hardest transition stage one can find themselves in. The reason is largely due to the vacillating nature of the grieving process. As mentioned earlier, grief, with its various phases, is neither linear nor predictable. I personally found, after my parents' death and during the divorce of my first marriage, which was collateral damage from my parents' passing, that I would jump around from anger one day back to denial then over to bargaining, only to find myself back at depression again. It was truly chaotic at times, with no rhyme or reason. Perhaps that is why this in-between place requires such patience on the part of the sojourner and compassion on the part of the onlooker.

Here we find the essential need to mitigate, if not eliminate, expectations entirely. Since the journey through the "valley of the shadow of death" is so very capricious and turbulent, one must grant themselves the freedom to experience whatever their soul dictates they will. Equally, a word to the wise: the loved one who wishes to be a companion, walking alongside, should take heed to allow, without criticism, such erratic behavior or deluge of emotions while maneuvering through the complicated maze of bereavement.

I was very fortunate, when I was passing through my grief journey of darkness, to have family and friends that demanded nothing of me yet lovingly offered all of themselves to simply be there. It was in this place of continuous encouragement to just be that I found the freedom to feel without condemnation or guilt. This is extremely important to take note of since the common misconception people experience while grieving the loss of a loved one, whether through death or divorce, is that certain feelings are wrong or bad. Feelings are neither right nor wrong when the tidal wave of loss is assailing one's soul. It is how we decide to act, as a result of certain feelings, that can be healthy or unhealthy—constructive or destructive.

Again, this is where we find the strength and comfort of sincere loved ones surrounding us to be of great protection. On the contrary, if one chooses to forge ahead alone through this dark forest bereft of solace, all the while giving way to self-condemnation for certain emotions and feelings, then that is a surefire recipe for thwarting the healing process of the wound of grief.

Speaking of misconceptions, an all-too-common one within Christendom is the belief that it is sinful, or at least inappropriate, to be mad at God. Certainly, I am not advocating or suggesting that we approach the Almighty in a flippant or disrespectful manner. However, to trudge through the grieving process attempting to conceal our true feelings from the One who already knows what they are is ludicrous. Instead, I recommend we approach the throne of grace with humility and honesty.

Hebrews 4:16 says, "Let us then approach the throne of grace with confidence, so that we may receive mercy and find grace to help us in our time of need."

I would liken this to when an adolescent tells their parents that they're upset by the punishment they have been given, yet all the while, they've been doing it with much deserved respect to ensure no additional consequences are incurred. God loves us more than we could ever fully comprehend; therefore, we ought to understand and embrace the safety and acceptance we can enjoy in His holy presence, all through Jesus Christ's atoning work on the Cross!

Remember Isaiah 53:5, which states, "The punishment that brought us peace was on Him, and by His wounds we are healed."

The following are not absolutes by any means; rather, these are merely suggestions for prayerful consideration. If one is experiencing what seems to be an inordinately complex grief, then *perhaps* it could be forgiveness that needs to take place in one's heart toward the loved one who has since passed. Again, this could just as easily apply to the loss brought on by divorce or an abruptly ended career. Forgiveness does volumes more for the offended or wounded than it does for the person whom we blame or perceive to be at fault. Letting go might be the precise step needed to move forward through the bereavement process and on toward acceptance and healing.

Then again, what may be holding one back, stuck in the mire of "ghostly" grief, is a need for honoring. Or perhaps it's the opposite, looking at the loved one who passed through realistic eyes rather than a rose-colored stained-glass window. As mentioned earlier, once I allowed myself to see my dad's shortcomings as well as his strengths, I found a greater sense of healing and freedom in my own life.

The key is prayer—prayer by oneself, crying out to the Lord for insight, wisdom, and revelation. And, of course, prayer by those whom God has graced our lives with. Psalm 23:4 reminds us, "Though I walk through the valley of the shadow of death, I will fear no evil; for Thou art with me; Thy rod and Thy staff they comfort me."

Chapter 6

Fallow Ground

If a person desires a beautiful garden full of vibrant flowers with brilliant colors or healthy crops rich in nutrients, they must first have fertile soil. No one in their right mind would ever waste good seed haphazardly tossed onto dry crusty soil full of rocks and weeds. To expect any fruitful harvest from that kind of planting would be ludicrous. That is the futility that Matthew 13 warns us about with Jesus's parable of how the farmer went out to sow his seed:

> As he was scattering the seed, some fell along the path, and the birds came and ate it up. Some fell on rocky places, where it did not have much soil. It sprang up quickly because the soil was shallow. But when the sun came up, the plants were scorched, and they withered

because they had no root. Other
seed fell among thorns, which
grew up and choked the plants.

Then Jesus goes on to encourage us that "still other seed fell on good soil, where it produced a crop—a hundred, sixty, or thirty times what was sown." So it is with our own soul. If one desires to yield a fruitful spiritual life, they must begin with examining the soil of their heart.

In Ezekiel 36:26, God promises those who are willing and obedient, "I will give you a new heart and put a new spirit in you; I will remove from you your heart of stone and give you a heart of flesh."

What a beautiful and hopeful assurance that our Heavenly Father can and will give us a heart and soul that is tender and open to receiving the seed of His Word and Spirit. To remove what is dead and so dry that it has become lifeless as a rock and then replace it with a life-giving, life-producing vessel through which His anointing and blessing can flow freely. This, in turn, is what gives the individual the privilege and honor of planting seeds in the lives of others within our sphere of influence.

Yet this miraculous occurrence cannot take place unless the soul is fertile enough to receive the seed that God wishes to impregnate in our lives first. Just as it says in Hosea 10:12 (NIV), "Sow righteousness for yourselves, reap the fruit of unfailing love, and break up your fallow ground; for it is time to seek the Lord, until He comes and showers His righteousness on you." It is only by seeking the Lord in continuous, sincere prayer and worship that we will see the fallow ground in our lives—the roots of bitterness, pride, envy, and malice—broken up and removed. Then and only then can we truly receive that which God wants to impart in us and through us. This, of course, takes time through a transitional period of growth precipitated by sacrifice and surrender.

But how does our soul's "soil" become fallowed? I believe it is a very pernicious work of the enemy, Satan. It usually occurs over time and not all at once, lest we might recognize it easier. There are many root causes, such as unforgiveness, hatred, pride, or even the more subtle jealousy and envy. Pride—which is, in this author's opinion, the original sin—can produce an extremely hardened and unfruitful soil. The reason I hold this opinion is because the Bible tells us that was the reason for Satan's fall and his being cast out of heaven. James 4:6 says, "God opposes the proud but shows favor to the humble." We never want to be in a place where God is opposing us. But rather, humble yourself, and God promises to lift you up (1 Peter 5:6 and James 4:10).

The main reason pride is an exceptionally common cause of fallow ground is due to its inherent trademark of not being receptive to any form of instruction or correction. Therefore, the only real way to counteract the residue of pride is to humble ourselves on a daily basis. It is not sufficient to merely pray the prayer once: "Lord, teach me humility. Help me to walk in humility as Christ did." We must be sedulous to pray that vulnerable and sincere prayer every day since the sin of pride is so ubiquitous in our society and in the human condition. As we open ourselves up to the humbling and sanctifying work of the Holy Spirit, we can begin to see the unholy roots in our heart's soil disappear. Always remember, it is better to humble ourselves first because if God has to humble us, it's usually too late then. The damage is already done.

Unforgiveness and bitterness are probably the next most frequent reasons for a person's heart to be full of unhealthy soil—fallow ground. The main reason here is due to the callousness produced within our heart from harboring offenses instead of letting go through love and understanding. I realize this is much easier said than done, especially when considering some of the egregious and even malicious acts that are committed sometimes, even within families. Yet we must recognize that to not forgive means we're giving the other person or the offense control over our lives. Not to mention the cancerous effect bitterness and unforgiveness can have on our health, both physical and mental.

Plus, all too often, we fail to remember the sobering words of Jesus in Matthew 6:15, which says, "But if you do not forgive others their trespasses, your Father will not forgive your trespasses." This is most definitely not a nugatory suggestion but, rather, a daunting admonition and command, with severe consequences if unheeded. We should always attempt to put ourselves in the other person's place and try to understand where the offensive statement or action is really coming from. Most often, offenses are either the result of the person's own pain, insecurity, and past issues unresolved. Or it could be a misunderstanding or perhaps a rigid expectation that wasn't fair or reasonable to begin with. I once heard someone refer to the "unholy trinity" as meaning the following: judgments, comparisons, and rigid expectations.

First, we have to understand that none of us were ever meant to be the judge of anyone. Prior to the fall in the garden of Eden, man and woman were to avoid eating from the tree of the knowledge of good and evil. God knew then that mankind was not capable of receiving or processing that kind of information without it tarnishing our outlook and opinion of one another. He wanted His creation to maintain a certain childlike innocence and view on life—hence, only eating from the tree of life. Ever notice how a child never seems to hold a grudge or offense toward someone for very long, if at all? They are always quick to forgive and even faster to forget, and they are most certainly open to accepting others with unconditional love.

Next, comparing oneself to another is a very slippery slope. It always leads to a lack of satisfaction and contentment. In a perpetuating cycle, we find ourselves chasing just one more—one more achievement, one more accolade, or one more change. The lust of the eyes and the lust of the flesh, in the end, leave behind a cementlike layer over our soul that prevents real joy and peace from permeating into our lives. If only we could see how each of us is a unique creation, fearfully and wonderfully made by the Master's hand, with special gifts and talents for a specific reason and purpose. Instead, we waste our time and energy in an unnecessary in-between place, climbing over that next hill only to find the grass isn't any greener at all. In fact, sometimes it's dead, as is now also what we left behind: the marriage we thought could be replaced, the career we failed to see was really our true calling all along, or the home we never realized was actually heaven lying at our feet.

Then there's the *rigid* expectations. Expectations, to a certain extent, are not necessarily dangerous or wrong. But when they become the master, controlling our thoughts, reactions, and motives, then they can become the worse kind of topsoil in our hearts. Topsoil that is full of thorns that hurt those around us. Thorns that end up keeping those we love at arm's length, precluding real intimacy and love. I believe this is the toughest to cure of all the culprits for fallow ground. This is where the "plow," by itself, isn't enough. We must first water the hardened ground with accountability and saturating prayer. Proverbs 27:17 (NIV) says, "As iron sharpens iron, so one person sharpens another." I love one translation (LSV) that says, "And a man sharpens the *face* of a friend."

That's an incredible picture of what accountability within a committed friendship or marriage is to look like. Just as the plow a farmer uses to break up that fallow ground won't be as effective unless it has first been sharpened, so it is also with our words. Since the power of life and death is in the spoken word, as the Bible tells us, we should always ask the Holy Spirit to speak through us with His life-giving, transformative words that will cut through the hardened topsoil of defensive attitudes, shame, or fear and expose what lies beneath.

Hebrews 4:12 (NIV) tells us, "For the Word of God is living and active. Sharper than any double-edged sword, it penetrates even to dividing soul and spirit, joints and marrow; it judges the thoughts and attitudes of the heart."

Lastly, grief, as discussed previously, is also a common precipitating event that can lead to fallow ground in our heart and soul. It is certainly understandable and not an easy one to fix either.

Since my parents' death was so very shocking and unpredictable, I began to insist that everything else in my life must be inveterate and always go according to plan. There was no room for change, spontaneity, or capricious outcomes. At least now, I am aware of this dire need to continually surrender this "thorn" to the Lord since He has already borne all our thorns in the crown of scorn He wore on the Cross. And asking those closest to me for prayerful support and accountability has helped immensely. While the grief journey I walked through, very slowly at times, did eventually wane and acceptance came, I have become exceedingly aware of the absolute importance of life-affirming relationships within the safety and blessing of family and community. This brings healing and sanctifying renewal. Then we find the fertile soil rich in nutrients and, in turn, can receive the seed of truth that sets us free.

Weeds of iniquity

So perhaps you've done the labor-intensive work of breaking up that fallow ground, and now you are enjoying rich fertile soil ready for sowing the seeds of life. However, you continue to see these persisting and menacing weeds in your life. These weeds are actually the reoccurring struggles with sins and bad habits you thought were long since confessed and repented of. This condition is what Scripture refers to as iniquity.

Iniquity is the residue from sin. It is the underlying proclivity to repeat an act or attitude that you know is, in fact, harmful for you, yet you can't seem to bring under full control. This is the phenomenon that the Apostle Paul referred to in Romans chapter 7. He said, "That which I want to do I don't; yet that which I don't want to do, that is what I do." Paul understood there are things from our past that are like hooks or strongholds that the enemy has established. And only God, in His infinite power and authority, can remove and destroy them.

I remember going fishing the first time as a young boy. When I caught my first fish, I was so excited and proud, I couldn't wait to take it home and have my mom cook it for supper. There were just two minor details standing in my way. First, there was this hook I had to remove. Now, as I began to fumble around with it, I realized it was in there pretty good, deeply embedded. And most assuredly, it was not going to come out easy. After about ten minutes of failed attempts to coax it out, in my youthful exuberance, I just ripped it out—along with part of the fish's mouth. Of course, the fish was already dead, but the trophy I would later present to my hungry family was certainly diminished. At that point, I realized it would have been best to invoke the assistance of my father, who was having no trouble whatsoever in removing his hooks from the plethora of fish he had caught.

So it is with these persistent hooks embedded in the fabric of our soul. There is only one truly qualified to remove them: the Holy Spirit with His faithful sanctifying work. Now, because God is a gentleman and will not impose Himself on anyone, we must, upon recognizing the need exists, ask our Heavenly Father for divine assistance. Just as my father, that day on the lake shore, was not going to deprive me of the chance to remove the hook myself, so also our Heavenly Father will graciously wait for our plea for help. It takes longer sometimes for certain hooks to be removed depending on how deep they are or how entangled they might be with other commingling spiritual tissue, such as "soul ties" from past relationships or word curses spoken over us. But once the hook is successfully removed, it is imperative we allow the Holy Spirit to heal and fill that area in our heart with His sanctifying presence.

This is the second step I referred to earlier that had to occur after the hook was removed from the fish's mutilated mouth. It had to be cleaned before the trophy could be enjoyed. This cleaning process is not always fun, and for a young boy, it was certainly messy. However, it was essential, for without the cleaning, the fish would never have become life-giving nourishment to my family. So it is with the cleaning God wants to do in our heart and soul, removing that which is now dead and spoiling and replace it with carefully prepared spiritual nourishment from His Word. We must soak in God's presence by letting His Word become inculcated in our lives. As we feed on the Holy Scriptures, we will receive insight and direction on how to tear down the strongholds that have kept us from enjoying life abundantly! Just remember, when those strongholds are vanquished from our lives, the space they used to occupy must be filled with something healthy and holy. Otherwise, we can unintentionally create a spiritual vacuum that could become inhabited by an even worse carnal, selfish desire or habit.

These strongholds are serious business and should never be treated insouciantly. In fact, it's wise to consult your pastor, spiritual mentor, or Christian counselor for guidance on how to pray specifically regarding this serious matter, as well as other ameliorating actions needed. It is most certainly a transitional period one goes through when the "old self" needs to be put to death so the "new self" can emerge. Please understand, the eventual demise of the stronghold has already been accomplished through the precious blood of Christ on the Cross and because of an empty tomb. However, there are subtle layers of unholy agreements we sometimes make unknowingly that are the impetus to a stronghold being established. These agreements—or soul-ties, as they are also called—must be identified, repealed, and obliterated first before the "strongman" can be evicted from our soul. Deliverance ministry is something always requiring prayerful, loving, and compassionate support.

Pruning is also an essential part of this. By this, I mean the willingness to get rid of habits, predilections, or even certain relationships that can give way to temptation, sin, or counterproductive strife. I once heard a pastor share a tragicomic story about a man who had struggled with pornography for years. He told his pastor one day how he wanted more than anything to be free from this destructive habit. He had tried every seminar and read every book he could find, yet he still struggled. Then, shockingly, he mentioned how every time he would walk past that adult bookstore on the way to work, he felt such incredible temptation. The pastor, upon hearing this, immediately offered a suggestion: "Take a different route to work!" Just as with pruning a rosebush, the key is to identify what is dead or dying and then remove it. Remove that which could contaminate other areas of our lives, if left unattended.

While there are certainly some steps that are quite arduous, we must take them to see real breakthrough. And there are also some relatively simple and easy preventive measures we can implement right away. Again, as with pruning a rosebush, removing the dead portions is a necessity to make room for new life. But don't be discouraged during this in-between place when what was once seen as alive, yet wasn't truly healthy, is now removed, leaving a noticeable starkness that needs new growth to be brought forth. This is where prayerful discernment and accountability from your closest loved ones will help sort out what should stay and what you should get rid of. Don't be reluctant to ask for this input. It is sometimes hard to see the truth for ourselves; having a trusted confidant with a more objective vantage point can make all the difference between growth and stagnation.

The question is thrust upon each of us from the Lord: How much do we want healing, transformation, and freedom? It is crucial to remember, what we don't deal with in our lives now, during these uncomfortable in-between places of transition, could very well be passed down to the next generation. For just as there are generational blessings, there are certainly also generational curses.

Children of Shame

Something there is that owns a
    child, that trades their pride
    for false guilt.
And perhaps for life remain
    beguiled, with fear misplaced
    and often built.

Their hearts lay burdened with no
    just plea, transgressions are
    another thing.
For that is guilt owned hon-
    estly, redemption paid for
    everything.

Yet tormented souls, morose and
    driven, their strength is spent
    on vain remorse.
And futile search for selves forgiven,
    martyrs by name though chil-
    dren, of course.
They sing their anthem loud and
    clear:
"I shall accept the blame for naught."
Though naught begot naught, and
    shame begets fear.
And children make poor scapegoats.

Their forbearers denied and refused
    to accept,
Their guilt and consequence.
Unwilling to own their err or sin,
Thus, offspring now to recompense.

For she is love unfaithful, and I am
    man once killed.
Each hidden stain and blemish
    truthful, a hallowed secret
    never willed.

Hence image saved and cherished
    dear, though casualties sur-
    render self.
Fettered by chains of shame and
    fear, for acceptance now deny
    thyself.
Yes, children make poor scapegoats.

Unaware of ghost in closet hid,
    'til time when all shall be
    revealed.
Then learn they must all shame
    to rid, with guilt returned—
    esteem thus sealed,
For children make poor scapegoats.

Chapter 7

Timely Tribute

This past year, a very dear friend of mine passed away after a hard-fought battle with cancer. His name was Dave. Seldom in life is one ever fortunate enough to meet a truly noble person. My friend Dave was such a person—a man whose character exemplified integrity and humility like no one else I have ever known. His infectious optimism and ability to breathe inspiration into a person's soul, motivating them to aspire to be better than before, all the while still making them feel accepted, was truly a God-given gift.

Even in the midst of a highly stressful and challenging industry (known as construction), Dave had an innate sense of what mattered most: the human element. He clearly loved helping others rise above the frustrating and even capricious aspects of everyday life to become stronger and more compassionate—a combination that is not commonplace in our society today. Yet for Dave, his inner strength came from his inherent ability to appreciate people for who they were and where they were in life, but he cared for them too much to leave them there.

Dave blessed my life in more ways than I will ever be able to sufficiently communicate. Knowing him as a trusted friend and mentor sharpened my character and helped mold me to be a better man—father, husband, brother, and worker. I will forever be in his debt for the way he poured himself into my journey of life. He truly personified the famous quote of Abraham Lincoln: "When we look for the good in others, expecting to find it, we most certainly will." That is Dave's legacy to me and to so many others who are better for having known him.

Another quote that epitomized Dave's life message was from General Patton: "Never fail to honor your people. When a true leader's work is complete and his aim is fulfilled, his people should say and believe, we did this ourselves." Dave understood the concept of honoring and affirming others. His self-effacing leadership style, leading by example and inspiration, will always be remembered and emulated by many.

The Bible verse in Romans 12:10 says, "Honor one another above yourselves." This was truly portrayed in how Dave interacted with everyone he came in contact with. He had a way of making a person feel they were valued, appreciated, and important merely by greeting them. His sedulous way of making time for others, whether it was an encouraging word of advice, a listening ear, or an affirming compliment. I marveled at how many times I was blessed to be the recipient of his life-energizing presence.

During the thirty years I was honored to be called his friend, I watched Dave carry himself with the utmost grace and poise through some very challenging times at work and in his personal life. Schedule changes, contractual issues, or other unforeseen difficulties in our business, as well as the illness he faced courageously head on—all of which could bring most men to a breaking point—only seemed to make Dave's light shine brighter. He had a truly amazing knack for seeing an obstacle or adversity as an opportunity to be even more optimistic. This was magnified by his intelligent and creative approach to finding solutions when others only saw defeat. His ameliorating humor during difficult times was always a welcome reminder to keep things in proper perspective.

I will forever be a better person—more hopeful, affirming, and caring—simply because of knowing Dave and being his friend. My heartfelt prayer is that one day, I will impact someone with the same probity and positive perspective on life. I thank God for Dave's life, his example and unyielding purpose, and for the impact he had on mine.

One of the many ways he impacted my life was shortly after we became friends and started working together. I was struggling through my own in-between place after my parents' death just a few years before and the divorce from my first marriage, which had just ended. Dave was there when I needed a friend to listen, to care and show support, and to offer advice when appropriate. But mostly, I just needed someone to be there. He truly helped me pull some deeply rooted "weeds" out of my life that were holding me back. And this, in turn, accelerated my journey through transition into a place of abiding peace.

Isaiah 26:3 (AMP) promises, "You will keep in perfect and constant peace, the one whose mind is steadfast [that is, committed and focused on the Lord in both inclination and character], because he trusts and takes refuge in the Lord [with hope and confident expectation]."

About the Author

David Mahan is a graduate of ministry from the Wagner Leadership Institute (a.k.a. Wagner University). He is married and is the father of one son and five grandchildren. Dave is also the founder of Ezekiel Prayer Ministries and calls Arizona home. His passion is prayer and worship, as well as American history. Dave loves to help others realize their full potential in God's calling for their lives.

www.ingramcontent.com/pod-product-compliance
Lightning Source LLC
Chambersburg PA
CBHW020641160726
47991CB00003B/972